Sharon Kivland

My father used to say that the finding of an object is in fact a refinding of it. My lover used to say that the refinding of an object is in fact the finding of it. My father never said that an object was lost inexorably, irremediably, no, nor that to refind the object means finding an object that is already lost. He was clear, my papa, that an object encountered once in the past, in infancy, will be later found again. My beloved, though, he said that objects were always already lost.

My lover paid careful attention to what my father said, and he listened to others, too, who also spoke about objects, lost and found, fantasised and symbolised, transitional and partial. My lover did not listen to me and usually I did not appear in what he said. My lover used to say to me, Your money or your life?, and then he would laugh, knowing that once again he had placed me in the position of a loser, whatever answer I gave. Sometimes he described the object, any object, as precious and gleaming. It was, he said, a votive offering with magical powers. Sometimes he said the object was like a plaything or an instrument that could be put to work to orchestrate a scenario of fantasy, where it would produce great excitement. He would look at me across the room full of people listening to him when he said provocative things like that, knowing I could not respond.

My lover never stopped talking about objects; what he thought about them kept changing. He had different names for them, for it (actually, it became one object in the end, one he called the 'little object a'), the thing, even in German, calling it *das Ding*. I could not understand much of what he said, especially when he started drawing algebraic formulations on a blackboard or went into logic or topology, with diagrams. I could not think all of these things together. Sometimes it was even a real object that appeared, like smoked salmon or caviar. In private, drawing pensively on his small cigar, a Cuban *culebras*, he would ask me to refuse what he offered me, for that was not it. Later he would admonish me, saying just because I asked him for something did not mean that was what I really wanted him to give me. It was easier when I was in my father's house. My father explained things more clearly. My father told me that we lose objects because we want to lose them, intending to replace them with a new object. My father helped me write about mislaying, and losing, and rediscovering, while my lover confused me, distressed me, with all his objects, those things that are not things that are found and lost and found again. I used to think about lost time, for instance, not to 'regain' it, but to free myself from it, to find the past to which loss testifies.

Having lost both my father and my lover, I mourn them, and it is soothing to speak of them at times. Sometimes I wear my father's old woollen overcoat. He wore it when we came to London. I slip my hands deep into the pockets. Sometimes I wear one of my lover's old shirts. I sleep in it or wear it to do housework. He used to tell me that desire had no object, and I think about that when I iron the freshly washed shirt, the thread of its cloth now worn, the collar, with its odd and particular style, now fraying, when I allow my hand to ran over its surface, smoothing the creases flat with my palm. I think about what it meant to be the object myself, an object, that is, for him, and I knew then and know now that love and desire are not the same thing. He would say that desire has no object or that desire disappears when it attains its object. Or he would say that an object comes in place of lack, in the place of nothing. I used to dust my father's objects: his lovely collection, all the figures, all the humans and the animals and the gods, their faces and limbs, divine ornaments. After my father died, for a while I would polish the little statues with my lover's shirt. I am a remnant left behind. Sometimes I have only a semblance of being.

My father used to say that it was a matter of indifference if objects were real or imaginary. He said that any difference only appeared later. He said that one takes objects in, and then one ejects them, and it was a question of testing existence if an object could be refound once again. My lover said that was a matter of judgement, always, and a matter of tracing, no, *retracing* a presentation to which an object no longer corresponds and to which it had once corresponded. He looked at me then and added, in a tone that was unusually tender, It is so difficult and detailed that I am afraid of losing you. Later that day my lover said that objects transform, are devitalised, that they are signs, that they are chased away when present, called back when absent, as a child plays with a toy, back and forth. And then, he said, it passes on to the plane of language, and that words are the thing itself, *la chose même*, he emphasised in case I could not get it into my head, not illusions, not shadows, not breaths. It felt -- it feels -- like a blind alley.

My lover said that my father said people engage with a quest for the object that gave them satisfaction once, repeating it indefinitely until they rediscovered it. My lover said that it was never the same object found, but simply a series of substitutions, and the repetition generated a world of objects. This world is not enclosed, he said, but open to a crowd of objects, which is functioning as symbols no longer even have anything to do with objects. *Oh là*, indeed my father would reconstruct everything, like an eighteenth-century philosopher, starting from sensation and going through to memory, stopping off *en route* at the search for objects, and returning, *faire demi-tour*, to think about sleep and dreams. My lover thought there was a secret confusion about objects, that they are taken literally and grasped objectively, and lord knows how one will find one's way without knowledge of the subject when one represents the object to oneself as homogenous with another object another brings to one. I was not really listening attentively to all that, instead thinking about the sign at level crossings in France that warns *un train peut en cacher un autre*.

My father said humans constitute themselves through the intermediary of a first loss. My lover agreed to a certain extent, nodding yes, yes, Nothing fruitful takes place save through the loss of an object. He thought the image that people (he calls them 'the subject', and it is a personhood, constituted by a scene of doubting self-affirmation) have of their bodies is the principle of the unity they see in objects, but it was sad, destructive, dehiscent, for they are separated from objects, which return in dreams as imaginary apparitions. People used to visit my father's house and over the wall, into our garden, they would throw scraps of paper on which they had written their dreams. Hah, all those fragmentary pieces of the thing in which they had failed to recognise themselves and where they sought to find themselves, scattered about on the grass for the maid and me to clear up, leaving the stones that were their ballast on the earth or on the path. My father placed great importance on dreams. An excellent sleeper, he dreamt of a book of plants, one he seemed to have written, a monograph with coloured plates and each page accompanied by dried plants;

he dreamt of his own pelvis and a portion of skin on the left shoulder of a woman; he dreamt of a grey horse with a leather saddle; he dreamt of some small curios shown to him by three daughters who were sitting on his lap. Yes, said my lover, reality is initially hallucinated, and he insisted that the end of my father's book of dreams implies that we remain suspended at the point of what makes our fundamental objects the objects of our essential satisfaction. Of course, my father said, we never do find again anything but another object that answers our needs in question. Indeed, said my lover, we never find anything but a distinct object since we must by definition refind something we have on loan. Meaning cannot be tied fast to anything and a dream does not reproduce recollections that make up the whole of its manifest content, what one remembers on waking.

My father thought that the behaviour of some people, call them hysterics, was intended to recreate a state centred on an object, the one that gave the initial experience of satisfaction. Hysterics fail to possess or have an aversion to their object, fall into a crisis of weeping, while others, call them obsessional neurotics, achieve too much pleasure from their object. My lover always said that it was a matter of organisation and the object, that first one, only shows itself when it becomes word, When it hits the bull's eye, he punned: *faire mouche* and *faire mot*. Both men felt desires could become tradable or saleable in the form of products. I kept my father's collections on my shelves after his death. My father said that a collection to which there are no new additions is really dead. His house became my house, even while my mother still lived. My lover was also a collector, but for obvious reasons (the presence of his wife, for example, or his daughter, or the interminable queue of devoted patients) I could not visit his apartment or consulting room, our intimate encounters took place in *maisons de passe* or hotels, and thus I never saw what he collected, though I believe he had some notorious paintings, including one that was screened by another painting on a little sliding panel, a painting that was an allegory of an allegory, leading to the drama of unveiling. He denied that he collected in imitation of my father. He kept a postcard my father once sent him. He said that an object in a collection is not at all the same thing as an object in psychoanalysis; on the level of psychoanalysis, one should not distinguish between a collection of works of art and a collection of dirty bits of paper. On the level of collecting, however, if satisfaction emerges from it, well, it does not ask anything of anyone. Yet he demanded a great deal from me. He did not hesitate to refer to me as the feminine object or lecture me on the duty of being the object of a loving passion, a spherical thing without feet or paws, a whole person that is the terminus of love and completion. He would put it another way: lacking subject, *erastes*, loved object, *eromenos*. He identified me with the object that I lacked. There were always shifting lines.

My father also smoked cigars, endlessly, until he developed a cancer of the jaw and a tumour grew in the soft palate of his mouth. Among the ancient objects on his desk, the figurines and little statues, he kept four heavy marble ashtrays and matches in a green marble holder. There was a cigar case engraved with a map of Europe on which France appeared in copper relief. If I ran my hand over it, it was as if France embossed itself into the flesh of my palm. My father still tried to smoke but a series of operations made it difficult for him to open his mouth to insert the cigar, and he was obliged to insert a clothes wooden peg to keep it open -- to make a hole. My lover said that mothers are the huge jaw of the crocodile in whose jaws we are held, and one never knew what might come over her to make her snap her trap: behind the lip, the fence of teeth and the bite. The object: a little wooden peg, holding the jaws apart. The object: a child, holding the jaws apart. The object: myself, between two men, taking me apart. My father said life returns through paths that are always the same, those it has previously traced. My lover said that is called surplus jouissance, like something one finds in Marx's political theory -- the difference between the renumeration from the sale of an object and what it cost to produce it, labour and materials, that it was a too-much of enjoyment, and begged me to bite my tongue. Everything has to be paid for, he said, yield and return on any investment (Rats and florins, reported my father, from another kind of psychic economy). At that time, my lover had started to call the object of psychanalysis the *petit objet a*, the little object other, and this little object changed hands, turned in circles between four formulas (though there could be many more in this configuration of the four variables of which his object was one, and a term he said should never be translated so it retained the status of an algebraic sign). He took out a bit of paper, Have a go, he encouraged, use a little grid called a matrix. Later he said we could know nothing about what determines an object, we could know nothing about an object, except that it is the cause of desire, a want-to-be.

My father gave intaglio stones set in rings to his closest colleagues, inviting them to become part of his inner circle, which later I joined to replace a member who died, one for another, a living daughter for a dead man. One ring was silver with blue glass intaglio, the stone was either first century BCE or first century CE, the setting, twentieth century, given to his friend. My father wrote a letter to that friend, saying that Forms may pass away, but their meaning can survive them and seek to express themselves in other forms. He entreated his friend not to be disturbed by the fact that this ring signified a regression to something that no longer existed.

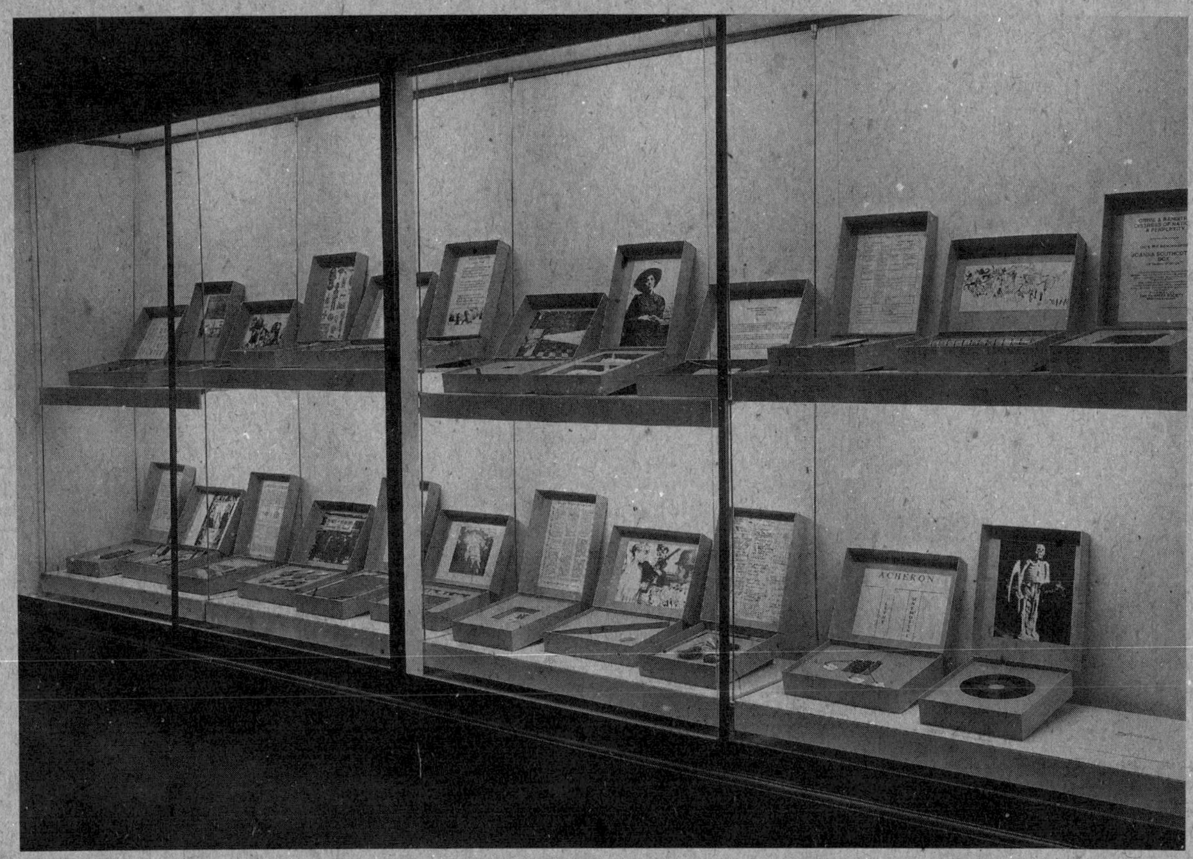

Susan Hiller, *At the Freud Museum*, 1994, installation at the Freud Musuem, London, UK

'Working Through Objects' is a text combining three talks given by artist Susan Hiller at the Freud Museum in London between 22–24 April 1994, and includes the audience comments and discussions which ensued afterwards. The text extends a mode of thinking that underpinned and shaped an installation Hiller exhibited at the museum that maps the boundaries between anthropology, art and psychoanalysis. The work was conceived in direct response to Sigmund Freud's former family home-cum-museum at 20 Maresfield Gardens and its once personal and then public belongings of antiquities, artworks, books and keepsakes. Ranging from the precious, valuable, sentimental and historical, to the familial and the medical, Hiller described the house as a 'provocatively poetic accumulation of contexts.' The intervention staged there was the first time the Freud Museum had invited an artist to engage with its collection and site, turning the space from an historical location into a venue for contemporary art and art production.

Titled *At the Freud Museum*, the outcome of Hiller's time at the house was a sculptural assemblage composed of twenty-three brown cardboard boxes filled with small selected items. Labelled, numbered and displayed, the boxes -- measuring 33 × 25.5 × 6.5 cm -- were installed in an existing museum cabinet built into one of the rooms at the suburban Hampstead home. Drawing directly from the world of archaeology, the boxes Hiller chose are the same used in the field for collecting and sorting finds. Presented in two orderly rows, one above the other, boxes were laid open to, reveal their neatly positioned contents, the objects inside juxtaposed with printed ephemera affixed to the underside of the propped upright lids. Set behind glass, it is a collection to be viewed but not touched. Eclectic in what they hold and show, the boxes contain the unusual, the profound, the mundane, the curious, the poetic. From trinkets to souvenirs, relics to earthly matter, spiritual mementos to everyday tokens, excerpted passages to black and white pictures, Hiller's assorted series encourage contemplation and imagination. To stand in front of them, poses questions about the specific artefacts and curios enclosed, but, taken as a complete work, broader critical reflection opens out on our individual and institutional collecting habits and value systems, and the way knowledge is received, exchanged, presented and shared.

Initially commissioned by arts publisher Book Works as part of their rich and expansive multi-site curatorial programme The Reading Room, Hiller's piece was later transposed from vitrine to page in *After the Freud Museum*, a hardback book published in 1995 by the London based press, with a second paperback edition in 2000. Following the artwork's first showing it grew in size, gaining further boxes with each new gallery installation to total fifty overall. Its name also evolved to *From the Freud Museum*, and the complete work was purchased for the Tate collection in 1998. Oscilling almost imperceptibly between the private and t public, the personal and the historic, the subjective and the scientific, it is at once the collection of an " and an "us", a highly subjective yet transcendental work. And these slippages and tensions are at the c of the discussion in 'Working Through Objects'.

Throughout, Hiller advances a context-spe approach to practice where an existing site is analy ally, critically and, above all else, inquisitively excav In so doing, the text situates the artist as a research and curator, as much as a poet and maker; two seem ingly opposing disciplines in art and science synthe into a single process. Rather than seeking hard fact answers, the results of such a method animate and evoke questions to be observed and sat with, quest that can seep and spread, finding root in other area of the mind. Made in response to the particular -- i this case, the Freud Museum -- the friction genera between the techniques, ideas and materials that w there before and exists now, can be productive and illuminating. As Hiller herself puts it in an afterwo *After the Freud Museum*, her collection and subseque book could have been subtitled 'sites of disturbanc A generative agitation.

Published here as a standalone edition, 'Wor Through Objects' is accompanied by two newly com missioned texts; the first -- a loose folded insert for slipped between the grey cover boards -- is a piece titled 'Little Objects' from artist and writer Sharon Kivland, whose practice considers, amongst many fuse things, the relationship between psychoanalyt theory and art; the second, a concluding 'Postface' translator and writer Paul Buck, who was one of Hi friends and contemporaries. Throughout the procee pages, supplementary photographs of archival mate taken at the Book Works archive run freely in gaps and spaces as associative links and leaps. To lift ag from Hiller, these image fragments -- much like th index of boxes and the multifarious things contain within them -- 'evoke moments of historical crises

This edition would not be possible without support and assistance of others. Thank you firstly Sharon and Paul for their invaluable contributions. to Gavin Everall and Jane Rolo for their encourager time and help. A special thank you and gratitude go to Gabriel Coxhead and the Susan Hiller Estate for continued input, engagement and advice in bringin this set of materials together and permission to republish the text. Acknowledgement must also be m to Barbara Einzig who initially edited this text and Erica Davies, the Director of the Freud Museum at time, who, along with Jane Rolo, the then Director of Book Works, and Susan Brind, organised the tal and exhibition in 1994.

Working Through Objects by Susan Hiller with Sharon Kivland & Paul Buck.
Published by Bricks from the Kiln (BFTK~WTO), March 2024, UK, in an edition of 400 copies; Edited & designed by Matthew Stuart & Andrew Walsh-Lister; Printed by Tallinna Raamatutrukikoda, Estonia; Typset in LL Ivory / LL Ivory Mono by Aurèle Sack & Marist Book by Seb McLauchlan; © respective authors; ISBN 978-0-9956835-7-0; www.b-f-t-k.info

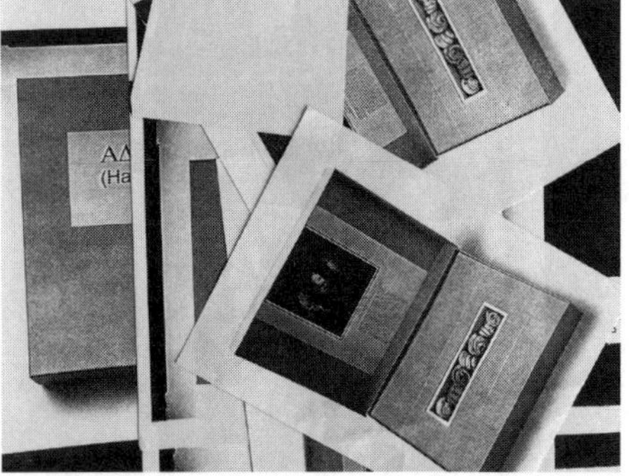

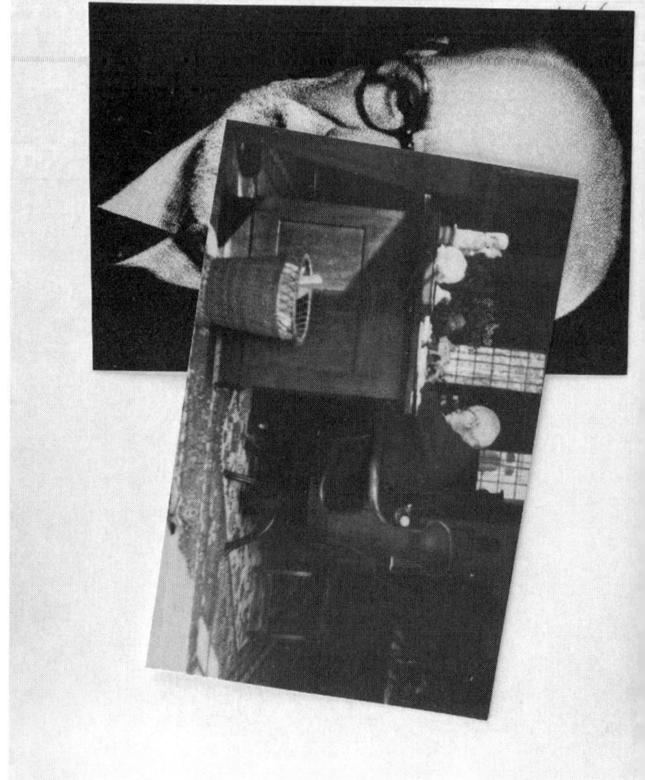

Working in the Freud Museum has been one of the most interesting
things I've been involved in for a long time. Most spaces that
one is allowed to temporarily inhabit as an artist are either
'neutral' spaces designated for art and thus marginalised in
some way, or -- particularly in Europe -- derelict spaces: dead
factories or abandoned warehouses. The Freud Museum, of course,
is quite different. This is a space which was a family home and
has become a museum -- or a shrine, depending on how you look
at it -- and which itself houses the collection of the original
inhabitant. So it has layers and layers and layers of meaning
in the present, as well as a very significant past.

Now my own experience here has been intense, probably
because working here has made me think again about issues I
thought I had resolved and to look at a set of histories I thought
I had already rejected. I felt I was constrained to confine my
intervention to the room where you now see the installation; this
may have been partially an imagined constraint, but nevertheless
I felt that my work in the space would be bounded geographi-
cally by that room. I also felt that in order to use that room
I had only two options: using or not using the existing large
vitrine. And if I had not used it, I would have had to block
off an entire wall, transform the entire architecture of the
room, and in a sense falsify the proposition that the room was
offering. Therefore it became a vitrine piece, but my series of
boxes was begun quite a while before the vitrine itself became
a possibility; when I was first informed of the vitrine I knew
immediately that this location would help me to finish the piece
of work that had begun long ago in my mind and which I thought
might go on forever.

The limitation of confining my installation to an oversize
vitrine in fact became a great opportunity, because I have discovered that when things are condensed or constrained like this,
people will involve themselves in a more careful, slow, and
intimate way than they do when they come into a space to see an
art installation which perhaps has spread itself out in a large
room where it is perfectly possible to stand in the doorway and
take a mental snapshot of the geography of the space and not get
at all involved with the items positioned within it. In fact,
and perhaps unconsciously, some artists now make installations
that can be summarised quite easily in a snapshot view. The
situation here is very different. We are all well trained to go
image by image or item by item through a museum case, and people
seem to keep this habit of careful viewing when they come to see
my collection. So I have had very full responses from people in
detail about each of the boxes in the vitrine, which is a very
unusual response for an artist to receive.

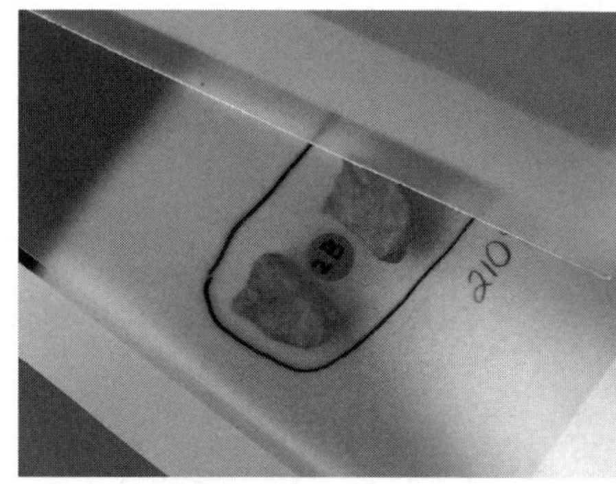

I take it that any conscious configuration of objects tells
a story. In fact, this is something I've believed for a very long
time. In the early seventies I made a collection piece called
Enquiries/Inquiries, which revealed quite explicitly, although
drily, in the style of the seventies, that any collection of
objects was an ambiguously bounded unit that told a particular story, and it was by setting the boundaries that the story
was told.

If you think about the narrative that collections or assem-
blages of things make, the interesting thing is that there are
always at least two possible stories: one is the story that the
narrator, in this case the artist, thinks she's telling -- the
storyteller's story -- and the other is the story that the lis-
tener is understanding, or hearing, or imagining on the basis of
the same objects. And there would be always at least these two
versions of whatever story was being told. This is why I value
the comments I hope you'll make later on, so I can get some sense
of what it is you think the story is. I have a pretty clear idea
myself of my side of the story.

Each box I've made and positioned in the vitrine seems to
me to be part of a process which is actually very dreamlike. I'm
again using the notion of dream in several senses. If you think
of Freud's notion of the dream as a narrative that had both a
manifest and a hidden content, this might have something to do
with the relationship between the story told by the storyteller
and the story that was being heard. I tried to make my boxes
exemplify that kind of approach, so that they present the viewer
with a word (each is titled), a thing or object, and an image
or text or chart, a representation. And the three aspects hang
together (or not) in some kind of very close relationship which
might be metaphoric or metonymic or whatever. There could be a
number of different kinds of relationships among those three
aspects. The 'meaning' of the entire bounded unit, of each box,
would need to be investigated by seeing the relationship between
the word, the picture and the objects, as well as by the place-
ment of an individual box in an extensive series of boxes.

Now in the Freud Museum we already have a complex situation.
We have a family house within which is Freud's own museum collection. To situate another collection here is bound to be make
it available to be read in the context of the primary collection.
This brings me back to what I said initially about coming to
terms with certain histories, with, if you like, 'the father',
here literally in the house of the father. The hauntedness of
this for me has to do first of all with my own gendered position
as an artist. Also, as I discovered, it has to do with issues
around ethnic identity, because my own family background has

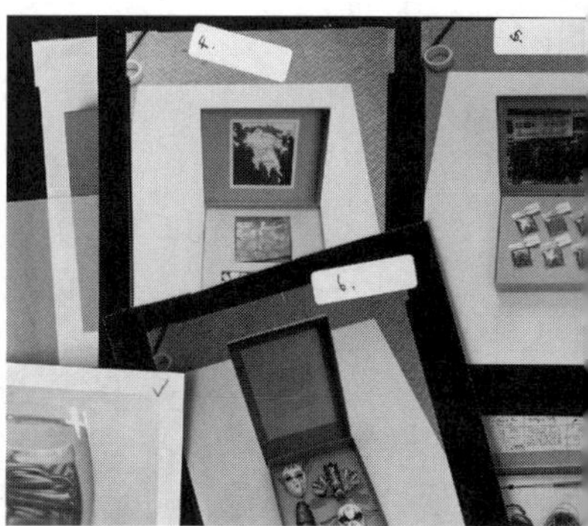

very much a similar trajectory to the Freud family background, and I found this extremely peculiar and resonant and personally difficult as well as interesting. Through this I discovered the continual abrasiveness of that particular ethnicity within European culture. In an art world within which ethnic identity is now one of the modes, if you like, of acceptable self-presentation which is valued, yet there remain certain ethnicities which are always politically incorrect. This was an interesting and explosive issue to deal with.

At first I saw that if I were going to compare my assortment of things with Freud's, there were some easy differences that one could name. For example, Freud had beautiful, classic objects which although not immensely expensive at the time he bought them, were still rare and valuable enough. Everything in my collection is either something that's been thrown away or is rubbish, of no value. The only value these things have is that I have assigned some kind of value to them. So immediately I could say that Freud is an early modernist with antiquarian taste and my collection is obviously very post-modern -- fragments and ruins and discards, appropriations, etc. So that seemed a good starting point.

The more I thought about it, the more I needed to think through the idea of collecting. A deeper, more distanced view reveals that the objects I have collected are constant evocations of mortality and death, which of course could also be said of the objects in Freud's collection and perhaps in all collections.

So there is a kind of circularity that I have discovered in my entire project. Any idea that I might have had about destabilising the notion of collecting seems to me fairly superficial at this stage and I certainly wouldn't have discovered these maybe deeper things, if I hadn't had the opportunity to work it all out through collecting these objects in the context of this museum.

Just as we could say that the existence of our dream life is a continual memento mori and at the same time an approach to immortality, since dreaming seems to have nothing to do with the necessities of physical existence -- so collecting may be the same kind of complex activity. It seems to be on the one hand the kind of sheer accumulating process that all children enjoy, you know a collection of dolls or little cars or comic books or anything like that, and then after that initial kind of accumulation children go into the sorting process in typologies, putting all the green pencils to one side and the red pencils, all the Superman comic books and all the Spiderman comic books, making categories and then some kind of analysis of these cat-

egories and all of that. It is a very pleasurable kind of thing
and certainly most people have done that, and then later at a
certain point you just chuck out all your collections. Usually,
you might keep your stamp collection because your parents tell
you it is worth money, or something like that. But you are fed
up with all that. You will tend to continue to define yourself
by accumulating objects, but in sets which are not really per-
ceived as collectible units. That is, you furnish a home or you
buy clothes, but when you arrange your clothes you don't put all
the red things together and all the green things together. In
other words, what seems to me to end isn't collecting but it is
the whole process of analysing, sorting and creating a typol-
ogy that is given up, because we certainly go on accumulating
objects which give our lives meaning. So I am maintaining that
the process of being a serious collector is very similar to
that initial making a collection in childhood. If you take a
real collector -- what I call a real collector like Freud who
annotated very carefully the date, the provenance, the price
of each object that he acquired in a very orderly and precise
way -- you can see that there is a tremendous pleasure there
that is taken, an intelligent pleasure in this kind of acquisi-
tive activity. The decision that Freud made to place all of his
objects in his working space, to create an ambiance that was
very different from the domestic setting, so that everything he
looked at in his office and consulting room was basically from
a tomb, connected with a dead body or a vanished civilisation...
Well, I think for me it would be a very difficult situation to
try to work at a desk cluttered with these immensely resonant
and haunted objects and yet I realise I am doing the same thing
in my own way. So I am trying to seek immortality and meaning
through objects and at the same time I am trying to say that my
own process of accumulation is really quite analysed and thought
through, and in fact is a critical homage to Freud and a form of
seeing through and working through. It has a double edge.

    First I'd like to talk about the archaeological metaphor
in my installation and to attempt very briefly to evoke a trace
of something of Freud's use of this metaphor, or more accurately
of my view of his use of it. Obviously, when you look at Freud's
collection of artefacts you see how important a certain notion
of the past was to him. He of course said explicitly that the
psychoanalyst, like the archaeologist, was reconstructing a
past through excavating fragments. He went on to say that the
psychoanalyst was, in fact, privileged over the archaeologist
in this sense -- that the analyst would discover a truth that
was more profound, because none of the fragments would have
been lost or destroyed since the mind never loses any memories.

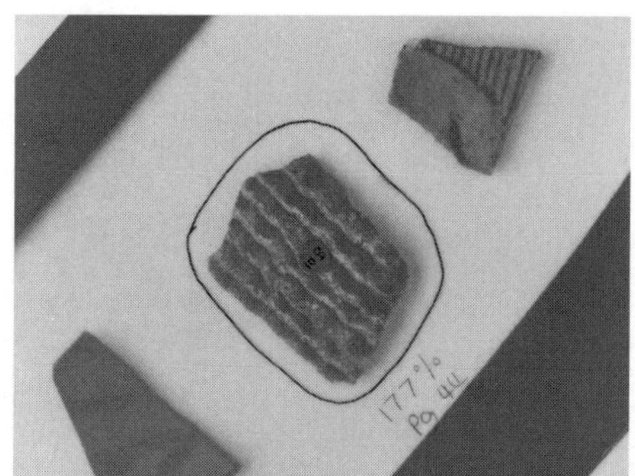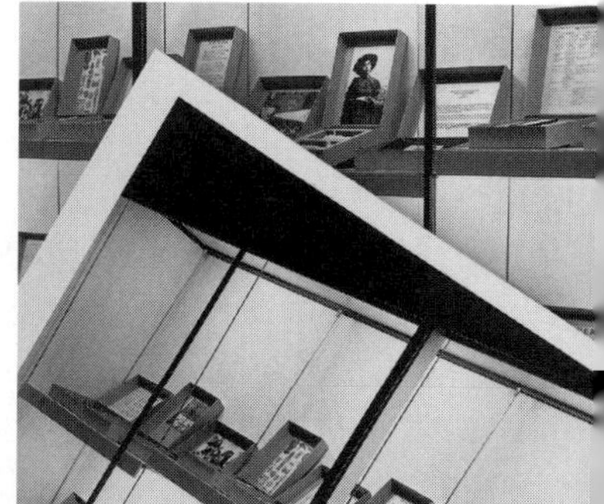

For me, having been trained in archaeology, I know archaeology doesn't necessarily tell any truth. It's a series of fictions, like any narration. We have a choice among these histories and fictions. Of course Freud had a different notion of science than we would have nowadays, of its offering the possibility of a unitary truth. This must have been helpful to him in giving him a kind of certainty within which to locate his practice.

I suppose I see psychoanalysis as more poetic than scientific, and in fact I don't even see a dichotomy between science and poetry. So I don't see any reason why I would have to establish my credentials as an ex-anthropologist or archaeologist in order to even talk about these things. However, my notion of art practice is an encompassing one. And my remarks around all of this are to situate the collection I've made within a discourse in which we could allow narratives of an archaeological nature to occur. One reason for raising the issues around archeology is to let you know that the boxes I've used in my collection are archeological collecting boxes, which may not be immediately apparent. When archaeologists do their fieldwork they carefully place all the interesting things found in a 'neutral' box. Then a series of hands-on acts transpire: sorting, cleaning, putting into plastic bags, reading, making notes and maps, even repairing -- I always enjoyed these activities. Out of them come typologies and chronologies. So by putting the remnants that I collect into these boxes I'm using the box as a frame to draw attention to something placed within it. Of course, a box isn't a frame, it's a space, and in that sense everything that I've done in each box is an installation within an installation. We're in a private home that houses a collection that had been annotated and dealt with in a scholarly way by Freud, and the house itself today is a collection of objects; even its ordinary furniture has now become museum objects. A box within a vitrine within a room within this institutional space within this house -- one is attempting to carve out a space in which something else can happen, to make some kind of intervention. So I've got a situation where I've used a preexistent vitrine which needed to be remade entirely, shelves, lighting, everything -- but in order to look almost exactly as it did before... Embedded in all this I've placed my practice of working through objects.

I thought I should say one or two things about one or two of the boxes to give some idea of how they put themselves together.

I'll start with one called <u>Cowgirl</u>, because that image of the cowgirl has become a sort of logo for my exhibition. The box starts with two cow-creamers, my attraction/repulsion for them. It's important in connection with these objects that I never heard a woman called a 'cow' until I came to England, so

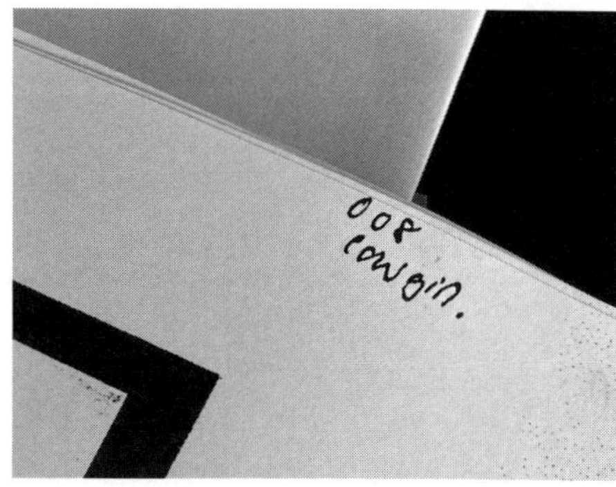

this is a box about sexual insult and my reaction to it. The
word 'cowgirl' puts the two terms together, and I came across
an old photograph of a famous woman outlaw/cowgirl; in the
American West all the famous outlaws and criminals posed for
their photographs, and Jennie Metcalf was no different. She had
herself photographed in her outlaw gear, and she's got a gun,
a big pistol. Of course this image was a totally irresistible
Freudian pun, and to insert it in the Freud Museum seemed to
me at first very witty. On that level I didn't see any more in
it. I put it together with the two cow-creamers (we call them
creamers in the USA, here they're called milk jugs, I know that
and it's interesting that both terms have sexual connotations)
and what I want to point out about them to you is that they vomit
milk, which makes them fascinating cultural artefacts. I always
think that the so-called innocence of artefacts is just a way of
letting ourselves as a culture get away with quite a lot while
pretending we don't know what we're saying. So putting these
china cows that vomit milk together with this armed cowgirl in
the Freud museum seemed to me a way of dealing with sexual insult,
and there was particular pleasure for me in siting this in the
house of the father.

Perhaps a sense begins to emerge of how they came together
for me and how I think they narrate themselves. The objects
within each box were the starting-points; the framing of the
objects, the finding of the right word or words and the finding
of the image, map, text, diagram or whatever, was a way of contextualising the objects, not to limit their meanings but to open
them out to these symbolic links along the themes I've mentioned.

One box that someone asked me about because I apparently
misspelled the word that titles it, and I do admit I have a real
block about this word -- the word is <u>Führer</u> -- there's a box
of that title, misspelled <u>Fürher</u>. You would think I would have
noticed it, which I didn't until this person pointed it out to
me. But in a way I am sort of glad that that happened, because
all the objects that I have accumulated are things which are
very very disturbing to me and in a way by making this kind of
mistake it indicates that the disturbance is quite real and I
am not just putting it on for benefit of actually exhibiting
it, if you see what I mean. But I think I have to say something
about this box. The box contains a book I found on a rubbish
skip and I had it bound. The book was published in Germany and
it is a tragic compilation of the history of the Jews from the
beginning, from Abraham, up until the year of publication, 1935.
It ends there. You can see the relevance of that to the exile
of the Freud family, the fact that they needed to leave Germany
and come to England.

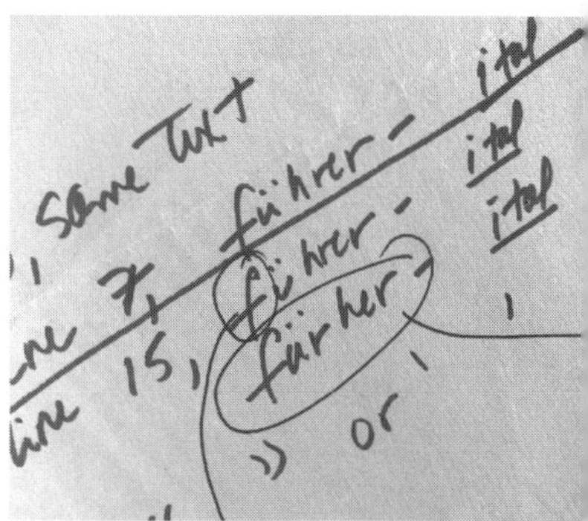

It's an astonishing book because the format is such that when you open it, you can pull out accordion-like pages that extend to become enormous charts that open and open and open. And that's another thing about the boxes: as objects they exist closed, and you have to make a deliberate act of opening them, just as you do with a book. Displayed like this, they're rather naked. But at the same time this display is limiting, because in many cases the boxes contain books which are meant to be taken out of the boxes, and read. Likewise, the slides are meant to be viewable, etc. So with the Führer box you would be able to open the book which is in the box, and open the large charts -- the book, which is about half an inch thick, in fact has a format that expands itself greatly. In the Introduction, which I've had translated and placed in the lid of the box, it says that 'this book is intended to give the Jewish people pride in their history and confidence for the future.' Of course, written in those years, it has a terrible irony. The woman who translated it for me said 'there's something intriguing here, the word Führer is used in the final sentence', and I asked what the actual meaning of the word was, and as some of you know, it means guide. So Hitler was actually called 'guide'. Now in 1935 the person writing this Introduction must have been using a coded language so that when he writes 'may this book be a good guide for you on the paths of life' there is implied a reference to the bad guide, if you like. And the accession of Hitler to power is in fact documented within the book, because it documents, alongside facts of Jewish history and culture, the main historical developments within western society, including 'Adolph Hitler comes to power', 'burning of the Reichstagg', etc., it's all there toward the end of the book. So all these layers within layers make this particular artefact very haunting to me. I called the box Führer because it all pivots on this notion of the idea of a guide.

Well, I'll say something about the 'Look Homeward, angel' box, do you remember it, the one called Heimlich? Many of the boxes use words from other languages, which is to give a sense of being outside the discourse, unless you speak the language. I've used some native American terms, Hebrew, classical Greek, Latin, German, French, etc. This is another German one, and it's kind of an homage to Freud, one of several boxes that make explicit reference to themes in his work. Heimlich, as those of you familiar with Freud's writings on the uncanny will know, is a very important word with reference to the German word unheimlich, un-homelike, which is translated into English as 'uncanny'. Heimlich means homelike, homely, cosy, from the word heim, home. But in Freud's essay on the uncanny he says some-

thing that in English seems very paradoxical, that the <u>heimlich</u>
and the <u>unheimlich</u> are very close. If you look up <u>heimlich</u> in a
German-English dictionary, what you find is that it says 'homelike', 'homely', 'cosy', 'comfortable', then goes on to 'private', 'secretive', 'furtive', 'hidden', 'forbidden', a range
of suggestions about what goes on and is protected within the
home, within the family, and you suddenly get to the <u>unheimlich</u>
without any break. You're led from cosy to incest. All those
meanings of home exist in English, but not explicitly, and our
word 'uncanny' doesn't relate to any root of 'home'.

In the box is a little 45rpm record I've kept for years and
years, of a song called 'Look homeward, angel' sung by Johnnie Ray. Most of you are too young to recall this, which was
one of the very angst-inducing songs of my teenage years. <u>Look
Homeward, Angel</u> is actually the title of a novel by an American
writer called Thomas Wolfe, at that time a very famous regional
writer. The angel referred to in the book's title is an angel
in a graveyard. And the home referred to obliquely is obviously
death. Of course this is not said explicitly in the song. So all
the teenaged girls were swooning while Johnnie Ray sang 'Look
homeward, angel', a song about death under the guise of love
or desire...

So I don't really want to say much more about that or any of
the other boxes except to say that each of them is put together
along the same sorts of lines -- following through on a set of
personal associations which initially for me were embedded in
the objects. I started with these objects and these are objects
that I have kept for years, little unimportant things, souvenirs if you like, with a lot of personal resonance. Of course
I didn't know what the resonance was. I just knew that I was
somehow stuck with these things and I never wanted to throw them
out. So I started to look into what the resonance of each thing
might be for me and then each got its place in a box and eventually I added appropriate contextualising material, a title,
an annotation and a date like a real collector would and that
is my collection.

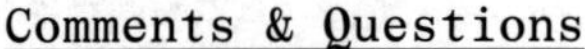

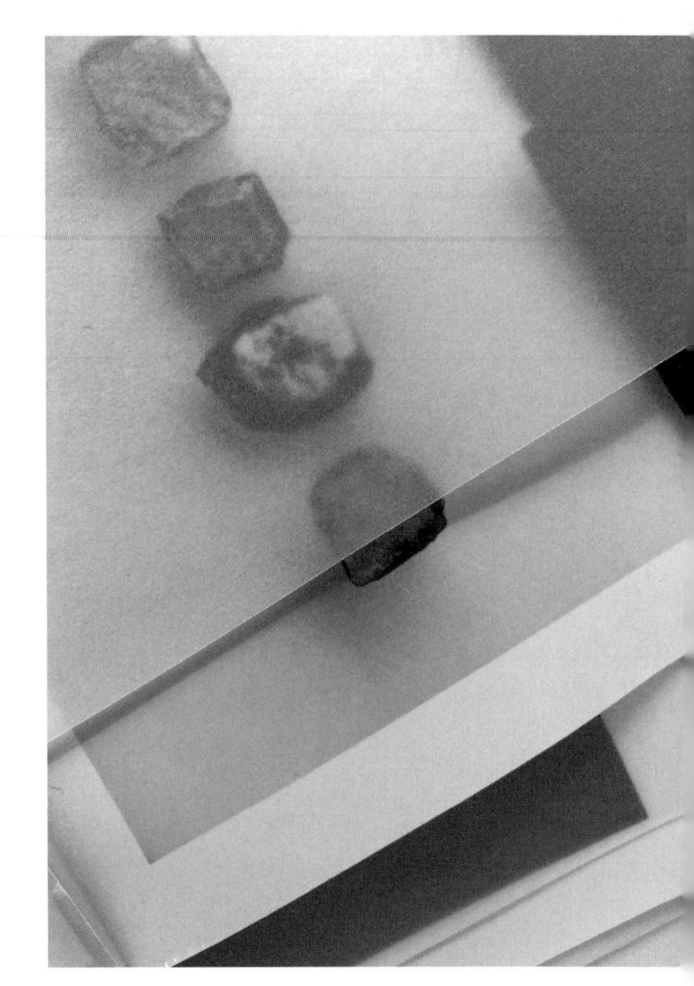

Yes. The thing is, just as with the *Cowgirl* box, I took
a certain amount of pleasure in understanding it for
myself. This point which had so eluded me in the past
when trying to decipher Freud's text on the uncanny
could be understood through objects in a different
way, so that suddenly I became entirely clear about the
heimlich and the *unheimlich*, the problem disappeared,
whereas before it seemed more of an intellectual para-
dox. In fact in talking with a couple of psychoanalysts
here recently about that box, I realised that it was
simply that people hadn't gone to the dictionary --
because it's still considered to be an ambiguous point.
I'm sure I'm making it sound much too easy; I'm sure
if you're a Freud scholar there are a lot more profound
issues around the remark that the *heimlich* and the
unheimlich are very close, but for me it's clear enough.

Yes. The context Freud's objects are in isn't just the
context of psychoanalysis -- the fact that he wrote from
the objects to texts -- but the context of a colonialist
European idea of availability. Everything is decon-
textualised and put in a situation of being possessed
by a European of a certain generation. Of course I'm
aware that even my collection could come to look like
that eventually.

Well, it is actually the water of Lethe. I do wish people
would ask me this more often because I feel rather
offended like Freud did if his collection wasn't appre-
ciated, that people would think I would have just put
any old water in those bottles. But there's more to it
than that. For Freud, his travels were pilgrimages in a
sense, far different from being a tourist. When he went
to Rome it had this inner quality for him. And I try
sometimes to have that kind of feeling myself, while
actually being of course a tourist. So I've been to many
places that have mythical significance, and the rivers
we're talking of are in fact magical because they are
'real' rivers at the same time as they map mythic space,
or consciousness. But of course to put water in a bottle
and give it a name is paradoxical because all water is,
as has been said, Ganges water... because all water is
circulating constantly. And there are other aspects of
my collection that are about these paradoxes, the *Seance
/ seminar* box with the tiny video: that is a collection
of shadows.

Well you know I did a box called in Hebrew *simchas*,
which means 'joy', which is what *freude* means in
German, 'joy'. So for me this is also the house of mirth,
if you like. One of the wonderful things for me was
that the museum gave me access to some very special
materials. The Director showed me a cabinet containing
a magic lantern and box of slides, which had never
been displayed or classified. Of course magic lanterns
have interested me for a long time; I did a large piece
called *Magic Lantern*, and other works of mine such
as *An Entertainment* make explicit reference to them.
In the box I made are replicas of these glass slides
from the Freud family. Glass slides break over the years
and you end up with incomplete sets. I catalogued
these remnants and found there were two kinds of
slides, the so-called scientific slides and the fantasy
slides: for instance, all the kings and queens of England
on a microdot, which projects as a blur unless you
have a really good imagination, and *Spirits Ascending:
Flight of Spirits Dark and Fair* from the painting by so-
and-so and that's also a microdot in which you can
see some vague fluttering shapes. These are next to
and completely mixed up with botanical slides, some
of which were beautiful ones purchased on the Strand,
and others homemade, of garden flowers. There
was also a set of Victorian glass magic-lantern slides
which seem to predate the arrival of the Freud family
in England but which have a number of English
themes: the British navy and army, British heroes
like the coastguard, firemen, etc. Next to these are
the earliest Disney slides, a sequence intended to
be drawn slowly across the lens in a frame by frame,
filmic illusion -- *Snow White* and an early *Mickey
Mouse*. This was all fascinating. On those long winter
evenings they watched *Mickey Mouse*. This added
another dimension to my thoughts on the father
and families because there's also a very normal side
-- watching television.

What I feel about my project is that it is to some
extent deformed by being displayed, even though
every collection is a narrative that wants to be spoken
or heard. But by displaying the boxes nakedly with their
lids open the meaning is changed. I'm not distanced
or dissociated from the familiar, but what it means to
keep the lid on is that the content is so Pandora-like
that it just might explode in terms of meaning and
consequence. That's how the boxes were made to be,
though here they seem as though they're making
some sort of objective presentation.

Yes, that's their original way of being, but not possible
realistically in this kind of situation.

Well, the point of specialist discourses is that there's
some kind of fantasy about them being more objective
and truthful than other discourses. As an artist
one speaks as a non-specialist -- I'm always affronted
whenever I'm called 'artist and anthropologist' as
though 'an artist' would not be intelligent enough to
have serious insights into anything, but an anthropologist or any academic person would -- whereas my
understanding about, say, anthropology, which used
to want desperately to be considered a science, is that
now they are all giving that idea up and emphasising
that they are writers of texts, of narratives, with practices that are subjective and provisional... I say to them,
yes, yes, that's totally obvious and has been for years,
but you're still miles behind where artists are in these
understandings and practices. You see, I think art is
epistemological, I think artists do address the nature
of meaning, of reality, and an enormous range of
ideas -- but always as non-specialists. It doesn't matter
whether artists articulate their procedures in words
or not; their practices are always culturally meaningful,
and that implies a certain kind of ability to negotiate
and transform fairly profound issues.

When I use words I always feel and always have felt
that I'm translating from something to something else.
At first I thought this had to do with gender, now I'm
wondering if that's all, or whether I'm simply the kind
of person who understands physically through my
sensory experiences, my tactile experiences. Objects
can provide me with knowledges of various kinds that
I can later translate. I'm not talking about object theory
but art, about getting your hands dirty, maybe being
stuck at that stage -- material practices. Words come
into it too, as in dream memories. I can't say what a
dream is, but a dream memory or construction might
be a word, a fragment of music, the memory of a colour
or a touch, a flavour -- but we can't dream without
bodies, as you know. And it's that level of embodiment
I want to emphasise when I say 'working through
objects'. Objects embody meanings.

Yes, the slides that can't be seen or books that can't
be opened. Quite. I'm very aware of that. The difference
between using and looking is important.

It's just part of the process of making each box. These
items were dated, these were assembled, these were
sorted, etc. In the *Fatlad* box, which says 'addressed',
this term is almost a pun. 'Fatlad' is in fact the Post
Office acronym for the six counties of Northern Ireland,
and it's how you can remember the postage for a letter

to Ireland. If it's a fatlad (Fermanagh, Antrim, Tyron
Londonderry, Armagh, Down) it's in the UK, if not,
it's EEC, for the Republic of Ireland. So when I said
'addressed', I meant the issue was being addressed in
that box, and it was also a reference to the Post Offic

This is always the point about art, I think. There is
a sense that all artists would like to have that non-
hierarchical, all-embracing, understanding glance o
the mother to encompass our work, so that we woul
need to explain anything or even to speak, but just
smile... One of my disagreements with conceptualis
has always been that I don't believe that intention
and interpretation are, or indeed ought to be, the sa
so I guess while doing the best I can to be as precis
as I can and to encourage others, say my students, t
learn to be as clear as they can, as articulate as they
I do feel it's essential to be honest. This means adm
ting that I don't understand everything about the w
and particularly not in advance. So my responsibilit
-- to use your term -- might be to function as a parti
larly well-informed viewer or participant, as far as
interpretation goes. I want the audience to be part
of the meaning construction, in fact I think it's alm
immoral to dictate their interpretation. Yet I will try
and try, to be as clear as I can. There's bound to be
some element of misunderstanding, whether or not
artist tries to censor it out as some do. There's alre
been some controversy about this current work, an
I've got to accept it.

I really work very slowly, you know. I've been think
about some of these points for twenty years. I work
from the notion of collections and museums in the
early 1970s, talking about fragmented discourses
and so forth. I also made a work that was a collectio
of cultural facts, very much in the tradition of Freu
collection of jokes. My take changes constantly, an
I recognise I am a long way from finally understand
what any collection of objects might 'mean'.

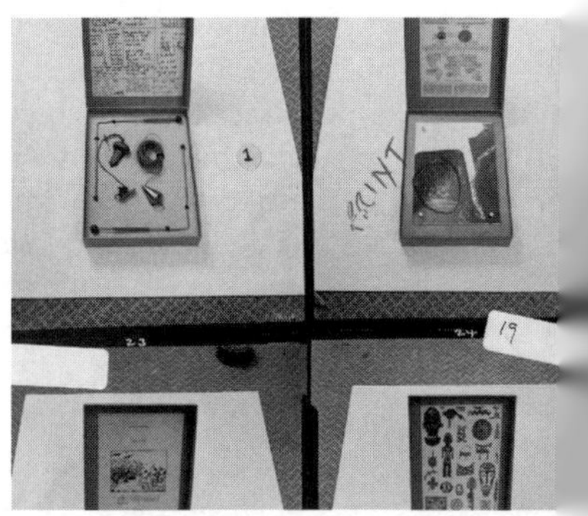

People seem to want you to fill in something, explain something, be accountable for meaning. I think what you are saying very clearly is that there are aspects of the work -- you have stories about them but you are of course not completely tying down the complete meaning of each piece and of the whole installation.

Yes, and I would go further to say what I've been saying for years -- that meaning is never fixed, it always changes. Not just as I make more work -- seeing meaning shift in past work -- but as we all live and change collectively. If we didn't believe in the possibilities of change we would disallow a future.

For me, the point of how you are talking relates to dreaming and dreams and the poetry of the classic. Dream interpretation never actually fixes the dream, that's doomed, and we all have dreams that we double back on and pick up on and we live that experience, we live it in our waking life. I think a lot of your work has to do with that, in relation to automatism and previous work, like your book on dreaming. So I personally think there is a profound aspect to refusing certain kinds of explanation.

Yes.

You obviously take anthropology as a resource.

No, I have been absolutely conditioned by it.

Well, that's what I mean by resource. Why deny other artists taking resources from other disciplines? This principle is fairly well established.

First of all, I spent about eight years 'doing' anthropology. I didn't just sit down to read one or two selected books about it. I am, you know, biased toward experience and I think the trauma of being indoctrinated into a, as we call it, into a discipline, is different from reading whatever you personally choose.

There seem to be some areas of enquiry that have a different idea of practice and competency. For example, you could say that reading through philosophy constitutes 'doing' philosophy.

Yes, you could. There are differences between fields of reference, obviously. Here in the Freud Museum, in relation to the experience of these seminars, I feel there is a psychoanalytic aura which of course has been used by various contemporary artists. Yet I really don't want to get too involved with that just on the basis of my reading, because I strongly, strongly dislike artists and academics using it when they themselves have never been psychoanalysed.

What I was meaning before was that the need for the discussion try and ascertain what the specific intention was, that also is part of making work. It is hard to live with this but we do want artists to be certain, clear-cut. I am talking about myself. I know I want that from work. Of course I don't get that.

I think you need to find a way through those contradictions you believe in, because if you don't allow art works their own space you inevitably reduce their activism. For instance, I don't mean 'vague' when I say 'poetic'. I want to allow spaces between the either-or you seem to believe in.

There are these contradictions in the practice of art at this historical moment. You know that I don't hold with definitions of the artist as someone who is untheorised and doesn't think. I don't mean that at all. Somehow in our culture we keep on making these false dichotomies -- painting equals pleasure, so Matisse is about pleasure and it's conveniently forgotten he was intensely interested in colour theory, he was not a speechless, anti-intellectual person.

And I also think you are saying there is a distinction between clarity and justification. If you are involved as an art critic it seems that part of that activity is to come up with an adequate theory or at an explanation which is appropriate to the complexity and contradictions of the work. This is the job of the art critic who tries different ways of doing that, but I think unfortunately art criticism, as some might say, is the last resource of the scoundrel. It seems to be the place for people who don't know about anything much, a place where everybody who has dipped into anything somehow ends up. So there is a bit of psychoanalysis, a bit of semiotics, bits of Foucault and Derrida all mixed up together. And then some critics want artists to speak in the same terms of reference. So it becomes all mixed up together, like a cake, and that's the interpretive model of the moment, which is what you are refusing to do in this discussion.

Yes.

I don't want to give you a hat to wear but in some respects it seems to me you would actually be more a modernist than a post-modernist insofar as -- there is, kind of -- I want to use the word 'hope'. There is a sense in which your practice suggests possibilities towards something, which is a defining feature of modernism as we all know. Modernism has theories about the future from which it understands and addresses the present. Postmodernism bans that for all kinds of critical and often good reasons, and in that one respect it seems to me a lot of your work actually is modernist.

Well, it has what look like redemptive aspects, but maybe I just like dirty, worn-out things. Schwitters' practice, of course, comes to mind, if you think that's Modernist, but I never think of myself as a Modernist. For a start, I'm the wrong gender. I would have no place within it and could never go back to those old assumptions. I think possibly you are a bit critical of mystical, utopian ideas about the future and hopefulness, whereas of course, having been indoctrinated within a social science framework I believe that the processes of change are embedded in the present. So it doesn't feel at all utopian to say that our practices as artist enable certain kinds of future to happen. It's a simple statement of a kind of social determinism, and I think we live in a socially-determined reality.

There is one box in the vitrine that really shocked me, and it was the one with the tiny LCD monitor in it, because I had seen the big version in your other show and liked it. I was very taken with the idea.

The big and the little.

<u>Yes.</u>

I thought of it as a collection of shadows: collected
earth, collected water, collected shadows. And of course
I like the idea of the camera obscura, the dark, the
dark room, the box. I called it *Seance / seminar*, to draw
attention to the kind of issue that has, in fact, been
circulating today in a lot of this discussion. A seance,
which is supposedly irrational and untheorised, means
in French 'a seminar', which we think of as respectable
and academic and logical.

<u>I was wondering about the relation of all these figures
to knowledge, because this has to be at the root of your
project. The figure of the angel is an interesting one
because the origin of angels is that they appeared when
men made contact with the gods, and the angel then
appeared as a creature which bridged the destiny of
something which was literally a lost contact, a piece of
something that could not be said, a piece of meaning
that was missed. The idea of the angel as messenger is
quite misleading, because it is not the case of a message
at all, it is the case of a communication gone awry,
but one starts and you have to finish it. I am wondering
about this gap and this kind of idea of knowledge,
figures of knowledge in those very objects you are
using: the angel, the cow, the home -- 'canny' in
Scotland is also a kind of knowledge.</u>

I don't think I could put it as eloquently as you,
but what I am suggesting is that knowledge is *between*
all these items, aspects, figures, symbols -- and I hav[e]
travelled to the ends of the known world in several
cultures to collect specimens to bring back to put i[n]
boxes. But it is not that, it's about what is between
the objects; context, words, history. In that sense
for me it is a fascinating project that isn't exhauste[d]
or exhaustible. The difficulty in speaking about
this is that it is possible to use up meaning by over
simplifying.

<u>I was just thinking about one of the boxes that has a[
little piece of marble... I was imagining it where it w[as]
originally and thinking about the meaning it had *in* [
and the meaning it has in here. I was wondering ho[w]
much of the meaning is already there when it is sitt[ing]
where it was.</u>

Well, you see, where it was isn't any place except a m[ere]
reference basically to the site of Hades, one version
of where Hades might have been.

<u>That is where you found it?</u>

Yes. I don't think I can directly answer the kind of
complicated things you are thinking about, but it d[oes]
make me want to say again that the interesting diffe[r]
ence of being a tourist or a pilgrim has to do with th[e]
inwardness of the sightseeing, if you like. One thin[g]
I always like to do is to have a kind of personal goal [in]
any place I am going to. A lot of the places I have do[cu]
mented or evoked in this collection are mythic and [in]
that sense part of our collective psychic map, the m[ap]
of our notion of consciousness.

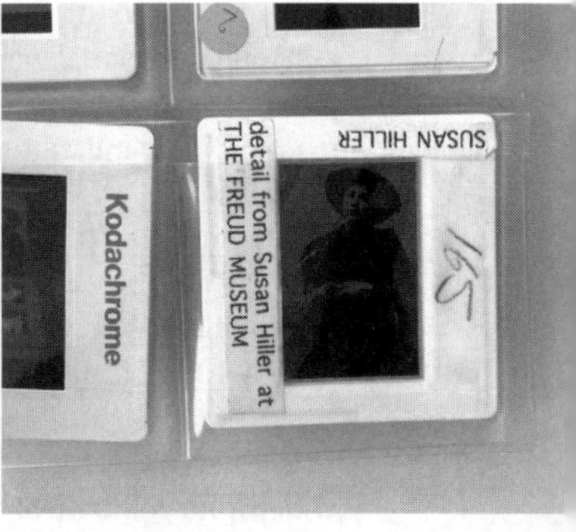

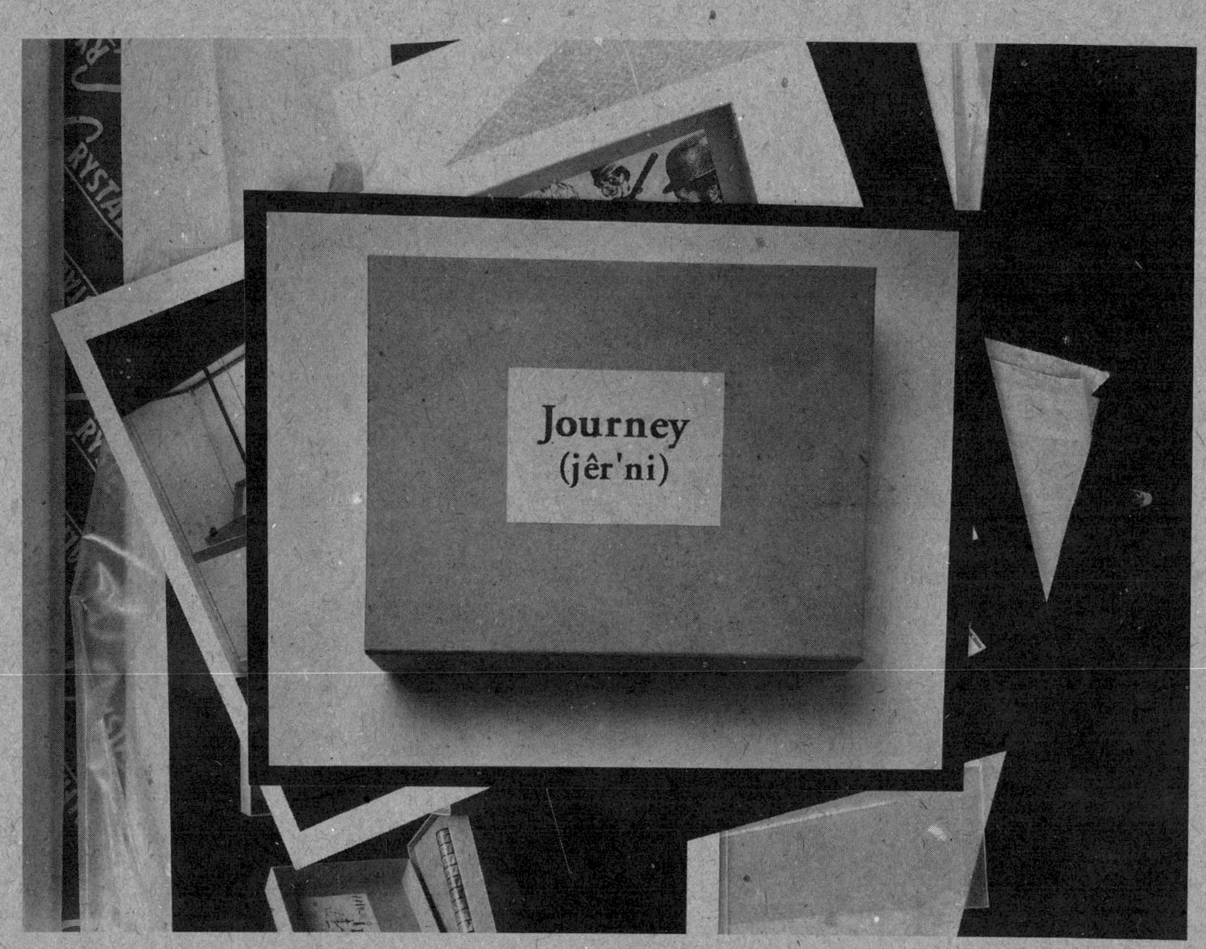

At the Freud Museum | From the Freud Museum stages of development:
Box nos. 001–023 original installation at The Freud Museum, 1994
Box nos. 024–034 exhibited at Gimpel Fils gallery, 1995
Box nos. 001–044 exhibited at Hiller retrospective, Tate Liverpool, 1996
Box nos. 001–050 exhibited in 'Material Culture', Hayward Gallery, 1997;
acquired by Tate collection, 1998

Bringing back memories, stories, anecdotes... and delving into any number of books and references of Susan Hiller's work creates a narrative, my own narrative, of how I wish to view her as a person, or give meaning to her work, for myself, my own being. There are many times I can recall her astute comments when we were together after observing an art object or hearing something said, whether on public or private occasions, and how that comment, subsequently buried, returns neatly to the surface for me to repeat and re-use, crediting Susan for having made the observation. I've done it fairly often. And what is remarkable is that I remember these comments so clearly, as if she had shaped and moulded them in such a way that they could not get lost or distorted, that they were ready for me to pluck and refer to when necessary. I can't readily think of other friends who have occasioned that incidence, other than my wife, Catherine. You'll want examples, but I'll refrain, because though I can build up a context to place it in, the examples work best in a particular situation, a moment where there is the context for applying it. Perhaps something will crop up here as I write.

I first met Susan in London in the late 1960s in a top floor flat in Moorhouse Road. I was there to see David Coxhead, her husband, and she arrived home during my visit. Over the years I saw Susan in various locations, sometimes with David, sometimes it was just Susan and myself, meeting for a drink or meal, visiting a show together, or travelling by train with her to view one of her shows, whether in Birmingham (*Monument*) or Oxford (*Fragments*), those two readily springing to mind. Or other times in London galleries. And also in her studio, whether to talk or to be involved in a project. And then there are the correspondence contacts, in the past my letters replied to on postcards, which have accumulated here, many with images of a 'Rough Sea' on the top side, Susan using the excess from her collection for her postcard series, *Dedicated to the Unknown Artists*, or excess from Rough Sea postcards that her friends and admirers supplied her with. In more recent times correspondence was by email. The only tool I cannot recall using was the phone, whether in the past, or in these times with smart phones. I prefer not to own one.

In the mid-1970s I contributed to the *Aura Series*. Susan held a blue glass over my right hand laid flat on a sheet of white paper and drew the outline of the radiating aura glow. She noted that it was strong between my thumb and first finger, barely dipped into the gap of the two spread digits. She suggested that this occurred with painters, who held a brush in such a way that the aura was intensified and highlighted at that point, whereas, as I was a writer, she thought all the fingers would reflect the intensity equally because a writer works at a typewriter. I explained that in fact I wrote with pen or pencil, and only later typed up the text. My main creative force flowed through the pen or pencil held between thumb and first finger. It is only in more recent times that I have switched to the standard approach of writing directly at a computer keyboard. As far as I can recall, I have not seen the results of the *Aura Series*, either noted in a book or in exhibition, except the couple of pages in the catalogue *Susan Hiller: Recall. Selected Works 1969–2004* from the Serralves Museum exhibition in 2004/5, where it is titled *What I See (the Aura Series)*.

Another time I contributed to the *Photomat Portrait* series. From her studio at the time in centra London, sited close to the corner of Shaftesbury Av and Charing Cross Road, Susan took me on a tour o the local automatic photomat machines, particularl row of booths underground in the foyer at the Leic Square tube, a favourite spot of hers, where we wor our way along the various machines, collecting strip of four that she later made into a *Photomat Portrait*. day the machines were well behaved, almost no tem peramental fits to miscolour or distort the portraits offer a different range of abilities in their performa Susan captured my wilder look of the period, where today I wear a more regular mask that seems to co my real face, the one of a subversive who has worke away steadily despite the inherent controlling proc dures of the system and its agencies.

Wedged among the books there's a large col lection of exhibition invitations and posters, assor notes and annotated drafts of texts or interviews a other ephemera dating right back to the 1960s. Else where there's the full nineteen pages transcript of 'conversation' that is considerably over-written and annotated by Susan, an extract taken from it for *Ce fold* in Toronto in 1979, retaken in 1996 in the collec of talks and conversations, *Thinking About Art*. The rewritings extend onto the reverse of the typed sh and give an interesting portrayal of how a conversa is developed into a publishable form. I note that th talk and subsequent discussions in this Freud Mu presentation is drawn from transcripts of three me ings, and thus falls into the pattern of how Susan always conscientious, always did something thoro once she was committed to it. There were no cutti corners. That would defeat the object. All was to be taken as far as it could go.

When I was preparing my show *In the disap ing mist, the gift whispers* at the Focal Point Gallery Southend in 2012, I wanted to devote one of the th galleries to work from artists with whom I had eng in one form or another over the years in my activit as either writer, poet, artist or editor. I asked Susar I could present a vitrine of her work, drawn from r archives, including some of the manuscript pages the transcript of our conversation. The success of vitrine I think drew on the way we restricted what was used rather than including too much, thus tak fragments of texts and highlighting them, enlargir them so that the visitor was drawn to ideas I want emphasize, not just left to scan and peruse a colle of open and displayed booklets or pertinent photo of her work. That way of presentation encouraged viewer to focus and spend more time by directing reading eyes. This is partly reflected in the subse publication *Disappearing Curtains* which retook th exhibition documents and reworked some of then in another way in order to explore in permanent f ideas around the exhibition. I have the idea that o the triggers for me is contained in a draft for a tal the Women's Free Alliance Seminar at the AIR Gal in 1977 that I found in the envelope collecting all t ephemera noted above. Susan writes: 'It is always question of personally following a thought, first i herent, later more expressable, through its proces of emergence out of and during the inconsistenci of experience, into language.'